My State

SOUTH CAROLINA

By Christina Earley

I0901984

TABLE OF CONTENTS

A Crabtree Seedlings Book

Crabtree Publishing

crabtreebooks.com

School-to-Home Support for Caregivers and Teachers

This book helps children grow by letting them practice reading. Here are a few guiding questions to help the reader build his or her comprehension skills. Possible answers appear in red.

Before Reading:

- What do I know about South Carolina?
  - *I know that South Carolina is a state.*
  - *I know that South Carolina has beaches.*

- What do I want to learn about South Carolina?
  - *I want to learn which famous people were born in South Carolina.*
  - *I want to learn what the state flag looks like.*

During Reading:

- What have I learned so far?
  - *I have learned that Columbia is the state capital of South Carolina.*
  - *I have learned that Congaree National Park has some of the tallest trees east of the Mississippi River.*

- I wonder why...
  - *I wonder why the state flower is the yellow jessamine.*
  - *I wonder why there is a crescent on the state flag.*

After Reading:

- What did I learn about South Carolina?
  - *I have learned that you can ride the SkyWheel at Myrtle Beach.*
  - *I have learned that the state animal is the white-tailed deer.*

- Read the book again and look for the glossary words.
  - *I see the word* ***capital*** *on page 6, and the word* ***palmetto*** *on page 12. The other glossary words are found on pages 22 and 23.*

SOUTH CAROLINA

I live in Greenville. Main Street has lots of interesting shops.

It is fun to go walking at Falls Park on the Reedy.

South Carolina is in the southeastern United States. The **capital** is Columbia.

Fun Fact: Charleston is the largest city in South Carolina.

The state animal is the white-tailed deer.

The yellow jessamine is the state flower.

We grow a lot of cotton in South Carolina. Some of it is used to make clothes.

Fun Fact: South Carolina grows 410,000 **bales** of cotton a year.

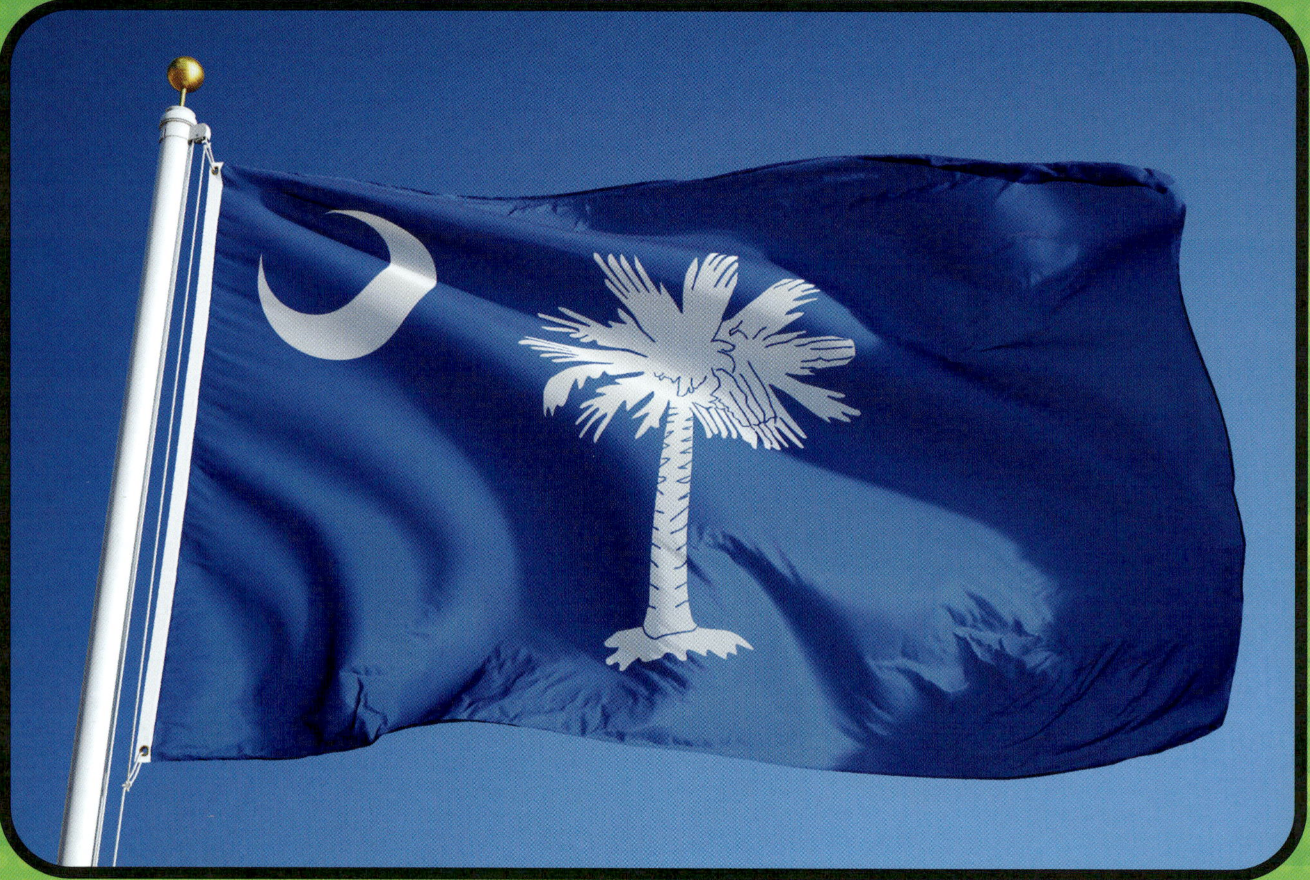

My state flag is blue. A white **palmetto** and **crescent** are on the flag.

The Clemson Tigers have won three college football national championships.

I like to go canoeing in Congaree National Park. Sometimes we see deer.

Fun Fact: Congaree has some of the tallest trees east of the Mississippi River.

I play golf at Hilton Head **Island** with my family.

I have fun riding the SkyWheel at Myrtle Beach.

Actress Viola Davis was born in South Carolina. Actor Chadwick Boseman was also born in South Carolina.

Fun Fact: Educator and **activist** Mary McLeod Bethune was born in Mayesville, South Carolina.

My favorite view of Lake Jocassee is from Jumping Off Rock.

Visiting Fort Sumter National Monument makes me feel like I have traveled back in time.

Glossary

activist (ak-tuh-vist): A person who works to bring about changes in politics or society

bale (beyl): A large amount of a material that is wrapped or tied together tightly

capital (cap-ih-tuhl): The city or town where the government of a country, state, or province is located

crescent (kres-ihnt): A curved shape that is wider in the middle and pointed at both ends

island (ie-luhnd): Land that is completely surrounded by water

palmetto (pol-met-toh): A type of palm tree

Index

About the Author

Christina Earley lives in sunny South Florida with her husband and son. She enjoys traveling around the United States and learning about different historical places. Her hobbies include hiking, yoga, and baking.

Written by: Christina Earley
Designed and Illustrated by: Bobbie Houser
Series Development: James Earley
Proofreader: Melissa Boyce
Educational Consultant: Marie Lemke M.Ed.

Photographs:
Alamy: Ian Dagnall: p. 4
LOC: p. 19, 22
Newscom: Kyle Okita/Cal Sport Media: p. 13
Shutterstock: Sean Pavone: cover, p. 5; f11photo: p. 3; Volina: p. 6, 22; Kevin Ruck: p. 7; Tom Reichner: p. 8; Chonlawut: p. 9; Serge Skiba: p. 10-11; Mark Winfrey: p. 11, 22; railway fx: p. 12, 23; James R Poston: p. 14-15; Natalia Bratslavsky: p. 15; PETER LAKOMY: p. 16, 23; StacieStauffSmith Photos: p. 17; Kathy Hutchins: p. 18 left; Tinseltown: p. 18 right; MarkVanDykePhotography: p. 20; Gabrielle Hovey: p. 21

Crabtree Publishing

crabtreebooks.com 800-387-7650

Copyright © 2024 Crabtree Publishing
All rights reserved. No part of this publication may be reproduced, stored in a retrieval system or be transmitted in any form or by any means, electronic, mechanical, photocopying, recording, or otherwise, without the prior written permission of Crabtree Publishing.

Printed in the U.S.A./072023/CG20230214

Published in Canada
Crabtree Publishing
616 Welland Avenue
St. Catharines, Ontario
L2M 5V6

Published in the United States
Crabtree Publishing
347 Fifth Avenue
Suite 1402-145
New York, New York, 10016

Library and Archives Canada Cataloguing in Publication
Available at Library and Archives Canada

Library of Congress Cataloging-in-Publication Data
Available at the Library of Congress

Hardcover: 978-1-0398-0534-7
Paperback: 978-1-0398-0566-8
Ebook (pdf): 978-1-0398-0630-6
Epub: 978-1-0398-0598-9